SHAGBARK

SHAGBARK

John Peck

THE BOBBS-MERRILL
COMPANY, INC.
Indianapolis / New York

Acknowledgments:
Grateful acknowledgment is made to the following publications in which some of these poems first appeared: *Antaeus, The Hudson Review, New American Review, The Quarterly Review of Literature, Salmagundi,* and *The Southern Review.*

"Afterward," "Death of a Stallion," "Hunger-Trace," "Leaving the Coal Cellar," "Søren," and "The Spring Festival on the River" first appeared in *The New Yorker,* and "Apple" in *Poetry.*

Note:
Several details in "The Ringers" come from testimonies in Ronald Blythe's *Akenfield.* The second colophon poem draws on the work of Roderick Whitfield. And "Spring Journey" may be read as a companion piece to the "Autumn Journey" of F. T. Prince.

The Bobbs-Merrill Company, Inc.
Indianapolis · New York

Copyright © 1972 by John Peck
All rights reserved
Library of Congress catalogue card number 71-187010
Designed by Nancy Dale Muldoon
Manufactured in the United States of America

For Alfred Kern

✍ CONTENTS

SHAGBARK

1

♫ VIATICUM

Shedding ravines
And mist shoaling the cirques
What we were has come with us
What we are hangs back
The sky waits for its thunder

Padded sticks at the temples
Our only rhythm
Then our guides calling
Small wishbones caught in their mouths
Gill pulse through a pine wind
That sucks at lichens and our names

Next they will raise their arms
To the last cols
Doors in this termless morning
Sills, thresholds
And the firmness beyond

And then we too can shout back
Toward the windlost faces
Ears waiting
Through involved porches and the blood within
Beachless interior
River and drum

Dust runs after the deer
Cloud prints the mountain

☞ ROWING EARLY

The mold-brown, moss-green, broad trunk of my wake
Spreads through trees mirrored on the morning lake,

And, through a wafer mist between the shores,
Grows bubble branches, budding from the oars—

Till it hangs wide and tremulous, and I
Stop rowing, watching it as slowly die,

Winking in rhythm—but the trees remain,
Imperfectly reflected, subtle stain

Deep as the sunken trees no one can see
That ride beneath us, like the green ash tree

At the lost roots of the world, in morning air—
Air quiet as this lake, trees everywhere.

The boat drifts on its image into theirs,
And they part to receive it, unawares.

✐ THE WATCHER

On the far edge of a plain,
As on white flats of Kirgiz,
A muzzy grey edge of men.

It moves in my direction
Through wind that sings.
An old anxiety
Relaxes, and I wait.

White-booted and white-coated
They approach over snow
That caves beneath them.
Their legs lift and plunge.

I am not seen as they near—
One speaks to another,
Confident, precise
Under white, fur-lugged headgear—
His language is alien
But I can see that he is
Confident, precise.
In my secrecy,
In my inaction,
I admire this.

Then with his trained eye
He turns, squinting above me
Into pines over my shoulder—
A flanking shaggèd wall
Over depths of forest.

His rifle goes up—
I follow its sighting

To a bird that perches, waxen
And with eye of dark berry.

As before, the wind that sings.
As before, a calm
Unaccountable, a moment
That continues to fill.

I do not ask, will it end;
But am aware of sky
As of scud over harbors—
Sheeted and stretched above
The snow poised on that bough.

✍ UNDER VIRGO

Farther than grass
might I go
listening

but for the
field's edge—
crud of gold

rubbed deeply
into the heavy
frame. There

rises the woodlot
and its other
whisper, its

browns and blacks.
Compost thick on
its floor—tasting

of brass warmed by
spittle, horn
pressed up to

distant lips,
embouchure of
praise, fat with

hope of harvest:
give it, bellower,
your high, firmest

tongueing, spin
the leaves into
dry light—

for they
forget you already,
the air has

gone shut
about them and
they curl, fingers

from cool hands
pendant along
secret flanks.

✐ COMING OFF THE WARD

These doors that kept the air so still,
Twin shutters over waterlife, tall glass,
Open with slow weight down the corridors—
They breathe out as I pass.

It was a light wind woke me here—
The bottles did not move in it, but hung
Bent windows in their saline brilliance, high
And quiet as my tongue.

Only the outer doors are huge—
They mirror street and building, walking men.
As you turn, leaving, you cannot look far
Back through their glass again.

And one of them swings out of phase—
Half of the mirrored street drifts into place
And then, without vibration, comes the rest
To meet it in a gleaming face.

✒ MAHOGANY AND GOLD

The doorknob, as you twist it, twists itself,
The door falls open by itself, breadslice
Tilting across the pillow air, a page
Spreading the odor of the long-shut book—
This is a room you lived in once before,
The paper combed out where you left it, food
Staining the plate with crumbs of shadow still,
Grainy beneath the glaze, your creekbed hand.
You wipe your fingers on the tops of books,
Part of the dust is dust and part is gold leaf—
You blow it off, snowing the slats of sun:
Which could be heavier in this quiet air?
A book lies broken on its spine, and deals
Pair after pair of doubles, like a choice.

ℐ DEATH OF A STALLION

Where malady has winnowed him already,
Sinking over the ribs into transparence,
He nourishes the foetus of symmetry:

Crupper and taut withers subside over bones,
Tail sheds the spent wave. But on two hooves he would
Fly, foreshank rising, rear shattering its prance

To cleave the grass of a gone summer. His head
Stoops, he studies the hoof he would lift higher,
And the hoof he cannot lift at all, beside;

Caught fetlock, the conundrum itself a door
To clarification. His separate eyes
Protrude to gauge it, his ears slant down to snare

Or brush it in passage, and they frame that place
Where the ball has entered cleanly. They would shut
Trim as the leather lip, they would shield those eyes

Budding like horns—incalculable velvet
Of the next moment, whose furlongs he has seen
Already, whose grass he has felt simmer at

His knees, running into that shadeless season
He would crest once more, rearing beneath lightness.

✐ AFTERWARD

We went as soon as we heard:
The road all suddenly
Lay puddled in headlights,
The pimpled skin of fowls—

There lay the outline
Of his body chalked,
Sprawled in sleep,
And of the flat
Flared oval of his hat—

To be cut out by a child
With snubnose scissors, and to fly
Crumpling in the soft wind,
Through the dark acre
Drift and spin.

THE SPRING FESTIVAL ON THE RIVER

Crowd fear: blown paper and uprooted ferns,
Down newsreel streets, down spillways,
Hands at random over me, cold pork,
Sweat runneling down my back—
Then the bridge:
Like carpet bulging up, it heaved the bodies
Wedging above the river, over barges piled
With cargo to the edges of their curious roofs,
Hulls squatting low into the water, swaybacked,
While on the bridge the heads bobbed like balloons
Between shops perched on either side—
Women holding their children high
Out of the surge, awnings snapping.
Where have I seen that other ashen whirr of images?
The public stairs at Chungking, after the air raids, after
The stampede crush—mothers as if asleep upon
The wide stone steps, their clothes torn back about them
By panic force of feet, their arms
Serene over the tiny bodies.

I cannot reach you now, how shall I find you?
Out of the back windows of shops quick with hands
Burdock and mangoes spill, the looser tiles
Like pebbles tumble off the eaves, and no one hears
Their sputter as they splash. Then, unmistakable
As bowstring past the ear, the whuck
Of separating cable. Massively,
Swarming with rucksack figures stabbing with long poles,
A barge piles out along the wharf beneath us, heeling
Into the current, its bow sucking fast;
The polers thrust, their mouths go wide and wait for sound,
Their arms stiffen, their poles bend, their arms rise,

13

Water spins its tons under sharp snailshell eddies,
The fine lines of that ink, how wet, how ancient.
Craning off the bridge, whole torsos
Lean down, grabbing stupidly, with knothole mouths.

I cannot reach you. Now it is I watch, farther along
The bank between two hulls, some boy oblivious
Who hunkers down, playing in shallows with a stick,
Picking his nose, poking mud into clouds of acid.
Now it is that dust motes, boiling into light,
Spin heliographs, but to what date, what hour?
The hills beyond the city: was it them I saw,
Glancing and running? Red, then, they were,
And silent: the bright and the clear—
Slabs of jasper, crystals of mica.

14

✍ THE HOBBIES

1

Boughs,
Traceries,
Riffle of sun.

Then grass,
Blurring the meadow.
From it,
Wind eating light:
Lime cold.

It draws to the rise,
Fronting a sky yet more cold;
Flickers in sleep.

2

Spilled strata, take them leaping
Flesh of the ball striking alternately
Heel and then heel following
On the stone cool of her porches—

Round her thighs these have parted
Thence to the sough
The young frogs not yet still
Her taut calves
Tugging at rooted mallows

Follow through skirtlash of pin oak
Fingers of shagbark—
These took her musk
The vial from about her waist
Catching and tipping—

It is here, unstoppered
Soaking the rushpath
With shadow

3

Old clearing:
Grass flaking to spikes of sun now,
Nostrils flaring with heat of that packed space now,
Weight of return that crowds
The fading trace of an unfound thing now.

With her it is an eye
For the first orioles
Distinct as dice,
Or for the hobbies, raptors
Of the agile swifts—

With her it is that rip
Of the air's jacket,
Bladefold of wings against the slategrey back
And plummet smack against the smaller bird,

Gripped now against
The black spots upon the white belly,
Tangled among the red ankles,
Folded tightly into that single sound.

16

𝒮 HUNGER-TRACE

Turn, let your nakedness reassume
The sun's body, let weight stitch your arm
With sleep: through you and under you, time.

Sand whelming dune grass, gritty flurry
Burying the small shoots to the knee—
Panic seeps from the body slowly.

And gull pivots seaward, steadying
Then yielding. Blade and wing hang planing
The one idea of wind too long

For the eye narrowing, tiring—these
Are receptacles, surprise gathers
Into them tense against vacancies,

Waiting till you wake. For then the low
Sound alters, light is newly hollow,
And the eye's quick lift its own shadow—

And the wing over you no reining
Hawk or falcon's, but greater, cupping
You in its air, freezing you how long

At the center, fresh crumb of darkness
Licked at by light: see the hunger-trace,
Fanning through feathers in a faint slice,

Slit of glitter left by lean feedings—
Waiting to strain, break clean and crippling
In the stroke downward of that still wing.

2

✍ THE UPPER TRACE

—for Y. W.

He was old but he paced
The both of us.
We followed the moraines
And cañons and the stranded rocks
A half day's climb, and then came on the ice,
A solid river bending from the col
Into its pool.
The high crevasse,
Cutting across the neck,
Held hollows. He went down
Past blue veins toward blue ice,
I following. The light was breathing,
Sleepily, as it does on sides
Of boats in rippled water.
Its wavering flush,
Unaltered at the fortieth layer
Of deeping color,
Unearthly on our flesh,
Wove with the sound
Below, a beating hush
Of water out of sight
Fissuring toward ground.

And he said, this is where the névé
Grips at rock and chokes with melt,
Falling away.
                    Slow cold
Had numbed our hands and forearms—
We angled back to the rim
Into shadow. It had come
Quickly, a wide half-cone

Fanning over us from the crest,
And it was this that let the white slope stay.

                            I asked

What is it throws the light back
In steady points from the valley?
He said, that is the sheer face
Of granite sliced and smoothed by this,
The tributary ice.
A horse strange to this country
Will smell the polished stone
And test it with his hoof,
Thinking it water.

We made camp, my hands stung
Back into feeling over fire,
Remembering sundered heft
Of things they made once.
Ruddy, the fingertips of pines,
Brushing the silence, were so steep.
His set face in the flickering
Wash of embers
Was yet the same
That I had seen,
But was as far
As it had ever been.
Dumb blood, how long warmed,
Reached now from my hands
Into my own face in a flood,
Barbed with sleep.

ℐ BROTHER

The light level, and all of us were there,
Dark balls clicked from the mallets, rolling hushed—
Older than I, you came back seldom then,
And when you came, came as you did just now—
Why have you come? Our voices gathered crisp
Through dusk of the garden, mingled, and were gone.
But you have come. We pull up from the lawn
The stakes and wickets, put away again
The pieces of the game. Then, easily,
Mount stairs to the upper yard, turn through the gate
And steer our faces through the solid light,
The wind floating our hair, our eyes half blind.
The old door waits inside the shadowed wall.
Within, the same chairs stand about the table.

✍ LEAVES FROM AN HERBAL

—for Robert Hass

1

So easily, the eucalyptus:
Broken across the spine or crushed
Between the fingers, like our tandem words,
Extravagant, the spearhead leaves—
They stain the wind with citrus while the grass
Crisps to a dirty gold and blows
Gulleying toward the Sierra, toward the lynx
And catamount and slope-necked deer
Wary about the salt-licks.

2

Sharing that oldest fear,
We wish to give each other still
More handfuls of that harsh
Persistent Spanish grass:
To thread the foothills, or go down
The Coast Range, or at last walk through the velvet
Defiles to the valley, once again to hear
That sound no other living thing can make:
A thin, unbroken tempering of the very air,
As of metal raised and shaken at great distance
Into the conch of space.

3

One summer I was hired to prune the grove,
Take out the lower branches and dead trees.
The seeds hung down in ropy clusters, brushed
Over my face, and popped clean in the heat.
I liked the stiff bite of the heartwood, heard

The back and forth stroke of the blade
Make the wet sound, acacia;
Saw thirty years go quick in the saw's kerf,
Whirled from the ripstroke, circling, to float down.
Then, legs spread wide, I bent
And from the standpipe took unbroken water—
Silvering off my jaws,
Ravelling into earth.

4
We crush the daily slice
Of wet fact in the mouth—
How can we know the shape that waste will take
At last, while now, across the nearer slope,
Brief cloudbreak spills its saucers of green light?
As if we could invert loss to look down
Its small end, aging already toward our gods.
As if these leaves could lose
Their incense, or the white ironbark
Its sweptwing veins, the same form young or old—
It rides air with the rippled sides of eels.
Think back—we stumbled blindly toward the pass
Beneath us, through chill dusk,
Cliff-brake wetting our legs, down through
The scalebark bodies of the yellow pine,
To come at dark upon the sawmill burners—
Bluntnose cones taller than full-grown trees,
Redder than carbuncles; and smelled
The pitch, alive, go acrid off downwind.

✒ INVOLUNTARY PORTRAIT

"Bad news," you said, and let sun render
The letter you unfolded brilliant with
The indifferent irony of natural splendor.

But then you turned, scribbled some plan
Across it, fixing fire in dead wine, writing
In time's teeth, as the unbaffled can,

Yes, countermarched whole seasons in your war—
Made spite and justice somehow both your friends.
All this I have admired, and more—

Yet, when you ask me to approve,
To foresee victory, I see instead
Your figure strangely set at great remove

Against a headland, posing there
Before my camera. And as I watch,
The focus will not hold you, and the air

Works changes like a fantasy:
Starts a scenario I cannot stop,
Gives me the island exile by his sea.

Fat sags along his poster jaw.
His eyes twist vacantly, regardless still
Of curlews overhead that wheel and call.

The cliffs march on the combers, deal
Their dull rebuff, and wait. Deal it and wait.
The curlews in their volley call and wheel.

And as he turns away,
The swift, high-angle shot of sentiment

Throws him steep upon the hill's flank—
His greatcoat slowly creasing grass, and bent
In the slightest parabola of blank

Intention. He ignores the road.
The crest might not be there. Below and always,
The slope-heaved billows stupidly explode.

 RELIQUARY

—for Jan Byzcewski

1

You walked into my boy's eyes with a cane
Taller than I, and tucked it like a blade
Into the stiff bow I could not explain—
Bonjour, smart click of heels, gloves of grey suede.

And when you visited you'd sometimes bring
Toy limousines rolled from thin British steel,
Or walk me to the low-roofed mineral spring
Edging the town, unfrequented and cool.

How could I know then what you might have been?
Or see, whenever it would snare your gaze,
Poland, and then Poland, or catch within
Your mild hauteur the diplomat's dry phrase,

Or know your old friend, whom you brought to talk,
Spoke almost never, hiding in this town
Simply to live, to dodge assassins, chalk
His cartel rakeoffs to the underground?

Your wife, the concert artist—every week
She came to play our spinet, having none.
Seated by evening windows, you would speak
With father over coffee, while the sun

Picked out her form beside you, fragile and dark,
And Cirisin Adamski, whose disguise
Of courtesy would focus so to mark
Some trace of Conrad quick about his eyes.

28

Old man, what trick has placed your relics here,
The ash of knowledge, and its little stain
Upon my palm? I watch them while the air
Interprets what their frail shape might have been—

Forgive me if I yoke the window wide
To let the chaff spikes of the amaranths
Splash rain across the sill, splash it inside,
Squeezed from the cloud's cold knuckles in a rinse.

2

The Polish cavalry rode quieter
Than any other. Down their roads of dust
Three inches thick, they'd suddenly appear,
Then vanish, gone before one could adjust.

This you had told me—this in lieu of all
You might have told me, all that would have seemed
Strange then, or even now, were one to tell.
I read once in Lednicki, how it came—

Half wakened by the baying of some hound,
He dreamed he was at Wilno, with the glint
Of fresh sun melting window frost, and found
His father trying to wake him for the hunt;

Across the snow hush of the fields he heard
The dogs like bells, at loose on the estate—
He jumped from bed, bare to the chill floorboards
And found himself, an old man, waking late

In summer, in his big American house,
Listening to a dog bark, far away.
He wrote no more. And if he were to rouse
Out of some other season, would the day

Fill with another light? You did not say
What happened when the life you had attained,

And Warsaw's skyline as you saw it play
Red on night's edge from your strafed fleeing train,

Had vanished into glare. Your wife yet shaped
Silence with lonely skill, and now I seize,
Guess at the hours she would regulate
With taut hands white and rapid on the keys;

Or see again, the day you took me there,
Adamski's yellowed rooms, and watch him trace
The history of those things he wished to share,
Tokens obscure with other time and place

✐ SMOKE AROUND THE BELL

1

Out of the tunnel to the last high truss—
Bringing your freights across the river
While the cab cleared of soot
You could lean out to see your wheels
Snaking the sun along,
Or hear, between the systole
And diastole of your lanyard bell,
The stroked bell on a barge
Bend down a twist of air.

2

You caught him in the yards—
The one who had smeared shit or cheese
On your boiler—
And you heaved him
Over your head, and threw—
And where he landed on the pile of ties
He lay in wrinkled sleep
While air stilled in the evening,
Cooling and settling. Then he moved—
You ran to lift him in imagination,
But you stood, feeling the ice, now,
Inside your ears trying to crawl away,
In sleeves and collar, and along your spine—
As the stick figure dwindled between tracks
In the punched gravel, never looking back,
The size now of your child.

3

The first one home had to go first next morning—
So you would sneak onto sidings
Shrouding your lights

And let the next freight highball through.
But while you waited once,
The frost, the hoar Altoona night
Froze steam-shunts under the driving wheels—
You squirmed between their flanges
Groping in darkness with a wrench,
Rapping along the clotted pipes and elbows.
One of them woke up, screaming
Its white scream, and you dove
For what you hoped was there,
That hole, man-sized, between the wheels,
And landed on the heels
Of your hands.
                    Late that night
You angled softly toward your bed
But your wife turned, and saw you loom
In your white windings,
And sat up quickly in her sheet,
Ghost to ghost.

                    4
You'd call, then drag on your cigar,
And when I ran in, blow it in my face.
I never told you, grandfather, how
I hid myself one night
To watch you pull your boots off in the kitchen,
Sing while the spigot chilled your smoky wrists,
And grunt a little as you bit the tip
Off one more, turning it between your fingers,
Sniffing it slowly while you stroked your back.

✐ THE BRACELET

—for Susan and Laura Chase

The unavoidable,
Said Edwards—that and pain
Give us back to ourselves again:
No gossip left to tell.

The personality
Is dross! We want the sense
Of proof, we want experience,
The pattern swerving free.

So mind seeks out its meat
Alive in the wide wood
Through brambles in the glow of blood—
There it must range and beat.

There—but here in my hand
Nestles what chance has laid,
Rolled silver, beaten to slim braid—
A young girl's bracelet band

Graved with an earlier name,
Six vanished girls before:
Edwards the pattern written there,
Rubbed to a low grey flame,

Persisting round the keen
Light wrists, the hair like down,
This bright cool circle round the thin
Unwearied pulse of sin,

Your own flesh young again—
Edwards, the pattern stays,
Alive and seeking sheen, the glaze
Alien from warm skin.

✐ OCTOBER CYCLE

Loons going now, whose range we lay awake
To guess at. Distances you choose, and lies.
Sumac ignites the path, and redwings take
The marsh again into their reedy cries,

And huts, abandoned, loom into their clearing—
Chessmen in one, toppled along the floor,
The board left clean, and rippled daylight tearing
Across the planking by the vacant door.

I set the pieces back in place, and watch
Light drift along the walls, feeling it cool
With its old auguries, while shadows notch
Around the pieces, touching in a pool.

Then I remember winter, how it fell
That year I tracked our stray foal through the brake—
I'd thought it was the same, late autumn chill
Till sudden snow revealed the icing lake,

Broad in the twilight, and I stooped to crack
Its thin glass, scattering the breath it held.
The foal stood waiting for me there, her back
Wet in the flurry, strung with blooms of cold.

✐ SØREN

The lion was his father,
   Apostate in the cage—
      A matted tail that swung
The mangy genitals
   Like severed fists; from these
      He saw that he was born
A moral hunchback. Fear
   Was everywhere, for fear
      Was thinking anyone
Might care for him, might love,
   Making him estimate
      His worth over again,
Even from the beginning—
   He who had no beginning—
      Force him to leave that room
Whose windows he had carved
   With his own hands, the door
      That only he could pass through,
The corner cot of straw,
   The lighthouse lens erected
      Gleaming in midfloor, naked,
The crate of notebooks scratched
   With clawmarks of Jerome's
      Blond beast, and marked *pariah*.
How leave those windows, marvels
   Of flawed glass, wart and wave,
      Each figure in sea change,
Tiding to petals through
   Disease, so that his eyes
      Wanted none, needed all,
Clawing gold from the canker—
   Hath nature fashioned well shafts
      Around roses, or planted

Roses in well shafts? And
   Who can uproot her dream
      Save he who dangles head-
Down in the cool dark column
   Of dead air, even where
      Narcissus died, and feels
The arrow from the god
   Sweet in his own flesh as
      He gazes at the buds
Sprouting in wall chinks—he,
   Who knew the god would shoot
      Sure as he bended down?

✐ LINES FOR LEIBNIZ

The hothouse flurry of the academy
Drove him to select life deliberately,

To let the carriage window's fluid landscape
Form his eye's garden, frame his singular grip

Upon the manifold—he would jot his notes
On whatever road sped the duke's business.

Those notes lie now in Mainz, Hanover, Berlin,
Ungathered. How long, in wood walks, had he been

Fretting retrieval of Substantial Form
Only to lose it to the leaves?—though in time

They gave it all back to him, newly perfect.
How many designs he left to execute—

Wagon wheels that plowed themselves out of mud, and
Nails whose tiny spurs lodged them unrepentant

In the wood, and a museum that would house
Dutch sail-wagons and Chinese wind-carriages.

But it was this gift of tongues made into hands
That fated him to build in the Harz Mountains

For the Duke John of Hanover's silver mines
A windmill pump, to keep tunnels clear of rains;

The delegation came for its inspection,
And that day the wind died out of all heaven.

The wind died out of all Europe while he wrote
To hold its unity before the breeze, set

Full above the signature, *Pacidius,*
To yoke schismatics once more in the embrace

Of dialectic, strenuous, with small spurs.
What years dwindling to carriages, those letters—

Yet, the acacia boughs outside my window
Do not sway in fantasies of knowledge now,

This time their disarray holds their uphill slant
With an old, unforeseen advent of poignance:

The fern accuracy of each tiny fan
Hanging from the haphazard inflorescence

Finds place in some unguessed scheme of completeness,
Though still I feel little toward this locust, this

Thorny tree of Egypt.
                      Morning: he embarks
on *postes 'portefeuille* for the petty and grand dukes,

Taking with him on the quick trip by carriage
The *I-Ching.* It is still morning, the image

Fashions him kin to us, yet remote as well,
A profile accurate and sentimental

Looking up from the series of charmed guesses
At nothing in particular, beyond trees—

He forsook religion toward the end. Only
One came to his funeral, his secretary.

✍ FOR A FRIEND'S MARRIAGE

Tall branches take first sun: she meets you where
   Your new luck like a match will flare
Most brilliantly, sure as its kindling sound—
   Folding its tip of light around
Your common hazard. Branches, and then grass—
   Your face is hers now, like the glass
Reality has fashioned, spare and grand:
   The sunburnt acres of your land,
Their canyon colors from the valley floor
   Shouldering the Sierra.
                For
Your own words make them mirror to your need—
   Your heritage that sweetest seed
Of moral arrogance wanting a place.
   Here you will bring her, where the space
Itself defines you, where great-uncle cleared
   White pine away and juniper
Through the grey winters of slowsoaking rain—
   Offering up each year again
All of his money to the land. He slept
   Always in makeshift sheds, and kept
His mute obsession close: he never married.
   But from the land itself he quarried
Chips and great chunks of glossy serpentine,
   All over a sensuous blue-green;
And set them by fine hand and Swedish eye
   Into the ramp and base, man-high,
Of his huge barn, that burned; and also laid
   That same stone calf-deep where he made
His roads, whose surfaces were terrible,
   But whose foundations let the soil
Breathe air and water and the roots of trees.
   All of his strength he gave to these—

Then turned, borrowing you to be his heirs
   At the last minute. So his years
Met yours—yours now the mare that would not follow
   Instructions, ghosting down to the hollow.
And stewardship held true—your family
   With almost Kantian purity
Took not a single harvest from the land,
   Learning to feel it in the hand
As his, even as cradled in the palm
   The sun warms it.
                    Often you've come
Out of the orchard into the lower fields
   And have seen, where they took no yields,
The brown earth rise through shadows of brown grass
   To meet the unmarked blue, each mass
Balanced against the others and their colors—
   Harsh to the ease of laborers
But generous to the eye, and to the land
   Solicitous. Each bottom stand
Of steeper timber he forebore to clear,
   And left to gather, year to year,
A grove crowning the hill for your home-place.
   So you have come up into space
Warmed by the dry uncompromising sun,
   And looking, suddenly gone down
Upon the earth, burying there your face—
   A simple and direct caress—
Not of the earth itself, but of that grace
   He gave it, weathering into place,
Outlasting failure.
              For the earth itself
   Wastes steadily away, down shelf
And steep arroyo, into valley haze—
   That is its nature. But the ways
He had with it, as light weaving the dust,
   Incredible, stand clear at last—
The lizard stroking distance stops, revives
   In that slow fire which makes your lives

The handiwork of passion, like his land.
    When the hot valley floor drives wind
Again up-canyon, may you taste it full
    As the tiny live-oak leaves, spread cool
And dark and multitudinous, still green
    In tuft and stipple on your brown,
That yield in quick vibration to the air
    And make one breathing everywhere.

 # WIDOWS

Meštrović

Hair drawn back close about their skulls,
They sit naked to the light; one falls
Backward to the other's gentle pull.

And sleeps. Her legs tilt wide, raised halfway,
Not yet old; they cradle vacancy
As they might a birth, waiting, heavy.

But the eye in her belly slumbers,
Her neck twists foetally, and she hears
The rush gather which the spillway slurs.

And she who holds her lets that head loll
Like a child's to her shoulder. Not will,
But weight in balance makes her equal—

Yet she is older in this grief, for
It is her hand twined by the fingers
Drowsing at last on the breast's contour;

It is her head that watches over
The sleeper's, her legs that splay wider
To receive the still form: —is it her

Own body that she props mutely there,
Mouth parted like her own? but no, her
Stare long since welcomed that other stranger.

ℐ THE FACTOR REMEMBERS HIS LADY

Gardeners kept these acres trim in my day,
Even during the war—Lady Ogilvy

Was newly widowed, but she maintained polish
With a force masculine, aye, bracing to watch;

So that now it is not quite regret I feel,
Or even the soft focus of unused will,

Seeing these walls thickening with the loose vine,
Whole prospects furry with grass, the pond unclean,

And the house itself wrinkling like an old coat
Over shoulders that are smaller now, that fit

Nothing they once wore—no, I feel otherwise,
Who managed her fields, affairs, and policies.

I can still see, beneath nets hung through her trees,
Squat bombers nestled in storage, tail to nose,

Waiting to jolt along strips near the orchard,
Often without lights rising from the dark yard.

It was she who ferried them. One night, past one,
She called me to come without explanation

Quickly up to the house. I went in my slippers
And met her as she came down the great hall stairs

Gliding with flashlamp past the high tapestries,
In flight suit, saying only that some malaise

Had stricken her assistant, and that while she
Could manage, no proper lady could simply

Go alone. So we flew where I could not guess,
Down between blue signals whose lanes swallowed us,

Then sent us back. And when I asked her what plan
She would follow were she to lose her way, then

She said her father once learned from his father
An oath in runes for entry into the core

Of their old wood; and learned the path leading there,
And learned the look of that hid place, forever.

And that grandfather had forgotten the oath,
But secured entry, remembering the path;

And that her father had forgotten the path,
But found his way to the place nonetheless with

Tag-ends of the vision, though the words were gone;
And that now she, too, though she had forgotten

Even the shape of that place, had not yet lost
The memory of the story, which sufficed.

✐ 3 ✐

◢ THE RINGERS

One day ringing men will be a race gone,
But how to picture it, that day when the land's face

Lies wildered of belltowers, its thicket of belfries,
Walls of poured stone heaving the strike notes sharp for miles,

And older walls of brick, powdery bisque to the touch,
Soaking up and sweetening the spelled sound.

And those rooms beneath the bells, walls like fortresses
Around the cockpits, where upward, through the embrasure

Dangling the great ropes, hover the dark zeroes,
Huge mouths all silent round their clappers, waiting for sound.

One day those men will vanish into their sound, but now
The troops of ringers come, bands of far walkers, hale gatherers,

Seekers of good towers, composers and turkey drivers,
To lift arms in those rooms, rank and captain, in array

Down the long ropes, and feel the fur ball of the sally
Lifting against the palm like a dog startled.

Thus, it was all that Bunyan could do to tear himself
Away from ringing. At first he came back just to watch;

But quickly he perceived the bells poised overhead
Could fall and crush him. So, he sheltered under a beam.

But what if a bell should bounce off walls, squashing him!
So he retreated to the door, shouldering stone.

But, should the shuddering thick walls themselves give in,
That too would be the end of Bunyan. He fled the place.

One day these ringing men will be a race gone,
As sun-glare drifts in curves over old blazons,

Or knowledge disappears into its overtones,
Or mortar powders grain by grain between granites

Rocking to tenor over Bourdon—crumbles as white
As it first was, drying spidery on the hands

Of masons who would sing swatching its cool weight in.
Until then, we can wait, busy this side of silence,

Imagining how bells might ring their own passing.
It used to be, with passing bells, we would go down

To tell the bees, so they would not die. When they swarmed,
The village ran out banging scuttles and fire-irons

Like bells to bring them down. And once, when the sun went
Into eclipse at midday, ringers were at peals,

Ringing through changes when the light began to change,
The huge half-violet shadow stepping overland

With noiseless speed, swaddling us in altered air—
And through that calm rose the confused cries of birds,

While steadily, those pealing Stedman caters kept
Time with their own time, ringing for whatever reason.

✍ CIDER AND VESALIUS

Like a fruit wine with earth
   Clouding its sweetness, color
      Of day's end, this cider
Collects light from the window
   Of October—I scan
      Vesalius the surgeon's
Woodcut anatomies
   Sliced and prepared for the eye's
      Terminal erudition:
This solvent ruddy earth,
   Chilled, is best commentary,
      It tilts the wings of bees
Into refraction, wings
   Already numb about
      The body of the queen
Who dies: long live the queen
   Bright milkweed drifts about
      Her dozing combs, the eye
Burs, rinsing her blind hives.
   We want no other gloss
      On this vivisection,
Yet want the litany
   Of fear transmuted, need
      The slow insinuation
Of spirits through our glance
   At knowledge.
           Look again:
   It did not move, it stands
At ease, it rises well
   Above the horizon, dressed
      In half its muscles. These

49

Dangle loose here and there,
   Rags in the white air left
      Motionless by the blast
It heard with ears it wears
   No longer. Now it waits
      Attentive toward the bright
Still landscape at its feet,
   The streets and houses empty—
      Its arm crooks in the quick
Arrest of intuition,
   Its finger lightly bent
      Toward a zone haloing
The smooth cope of the skull
   Whose back is all we see,
      White, blooming suddenly
Out of the sinuous stem
   Sheathing the spine. Now, soon,
      That silver sound again—

These streets are some real city,
   No Hieronymus Bosch
      Weaving his figures here,
Arguing brutal and
   Sophisticated joy
      Behind the passionless
And naked faces, through
   Steel wires penetrating
      The body pinioned by
The harp in hell. Threads tensile,
   Demons reaching to pluck
      And stroke them into music,
For we sing without joy
   Or knowledge, bone against
      Muscle, muscle against
Nerve and vessel.
             The young
   Student went from Louvain
      Out to the roadside gibbet

Late at night, and he pulled
    The femur off the hip—
        The bones were bare, still joined
By ligaments—and then
    Each night thereafter, piece
        By piece, till finally
Only the thorax hung
    From its chain. His desire
        Was great: he clambered up
And yanked it off, and made
    His first articulated
        Skeleton. Then he said
Discreetly that he'd bought
    The thing in Paris.
                    But
        The first plates that he made
Were thumbed so avidly
    That they disintegrated.
        And all his woodcut blocks
Were lugged across the Alps,
    Over half Germany,
        Outliving half a dozen
Publishers. Now it rests
    With us to speak the sequel
        As if to his portrait, where
He holds the malefactor's
    Dissected hand, each tendon
        Strung out in demonstration—
We must tell him the hand
    Has not changed, it is still
        The malefactor's, and
It is alive. The pale
    Tendons have reacquired
        Occulted vigor, slipped
Back into place, and bathed
    In blood again, that blood
        Which in all innocence,

At freezing altitude,
    Required the flier's glove
        Of fur and swarthy leather.
Over the skies of Munich,
    Through searchlights sweeping cloud
        And flak flowers, that hand
Squeezed its release, and all
    The fine grain of our shape
        Graved deep into your blocks
Of oak, the arteries
    Feeding back to the great
        Aorta, *toti corpori*
vitalem spiritum—
    All melted in the sudden
        Flame—*naturalemque*
calorem.
                This is the
    Last glass, spinning its lees
        To hellswirls out of Bosch
In silence, emptying
    Its far end, tunnel of spirits,
        Bosch's ascension panel—
Inexplicably yours,
    Who wait there with the other
        Suspect seekers for escort,
Angels handing you on
    With your face passionless
        And final toward the mouth
Of the high tunnel, till
    You travel where the shapes
        In little pairs waft lightward,
Mount through to the other side.
    With us you leave these other
        Figures, diagrams
Of unwilled ecstasy,
    Sinews drying to ink,
        This glass drying to stains

Of cider, while the autumn
   Milkweed lifts into air,
     Silk wrinkling in wind,
White inchworms draped from trees
   At loose in the loose wind,
     Fouling whatever moves,
Squandering transformation.

𝒞 COLOPHON FOR LAN-T'ING HSIU-HSI
(The Gathering at the Orchid Pavilion by Ch'ien Ku, 16th Century)

This is no poet's heaven
Where solitaries stroll the boulevards
Drunk with the power of transformation,
But a piece of earth near Shanyin
With a dragon-vein brook curving through it
And orchid, bamboo, pine, and one old ginkgo
Making a pavilion at Lan t'ing.
Attendants glide along the bankside paths
Carrying salvers of fresh handscrolls
Tied up in fascicles
To figures ranged along the banks
Seated in lotus-fashion.
Other attendants settle cups of wine
On pads of lotus where the stream begins
And set them all adrift—
Each poet, with his stick,
Must capture one of these, drain off the cup,
And, as he may, submit thus to invention,
In solitude or conversation.
Those who can write no lines
Must drink off three whole cups
And place the empty vessels
On a tray, drying toward their glaze,
In a neat row set them down.
One man leans on his shoulder toward the stream
And vacantly regards the cups
Slide past him on the indolent current:
The wine tosses the same light
That the water tosses.

54

Others unroll their scrolls
And display to themselves
The white space that is theirs.
Framed in the keyhole of a tunnel rock
Another stares at the brook,
His hand extended in rhetorical stasis.
And so, down through the garden, each in place—
With their thin wands
They fish for cups and poems, or prod them past
The reach of their own hands.
One of them drinks, he rises into dance,
A dewlap bear in silks!
His hands hunt halfway up his fanning sleeves—
While on the other shore his neighbor
Squats in frustration.
And the last figure, who has drunk his three
Already, and need take no more,
Reaches to catch one cup that would float free—
For just at this point the pavilion ends,
The stream now widens and descends
Toward houses and sheaf-bearing men
Half-visible through trees or down ravines—
And all the undrunk poems, the chill wine,
Must be retrieved, and gathered on red trays.
And yet, beyond the farthest trees
And left edge of the painting with its seals,
Come poems themselves—
The ones composed that day, with all the names
Of those who failed,
Full thirty feet of scroll spilling
Downstream into the world—

> For so it is with all men: a little while
> In good talk or high feeling,
> A little while
> With no mind for our end.
> But then sharply it comes

Back in upon us.
The dead felt as we do,
Read them:
Just so shall we be read.
Therefore my notes on this feast,
These poems,
            I, Wang Hsi-chih.

COLOPHON FOR CH'ING-MING SHANG-HO T'U
(The Ch'ing-ming Festival at the River by Chang Tse-tuan, 12th Century)

The woodsmen yank their donkeys
Heavy with cuttings
Out of the misty wood.
The hamlet sleeps, empty as the crows' nests.
Willows stain first light with celery tips.

Through them a family entourage
Returns from the ancestral tombs:
The foremost horseman leans
Outward in gallop, catching
Sight of the city—
His cries would leave his mouth
With the clarity of vision
Were not his form rubbed clean away by time.
The others lope behind him
Even sedan carriers
Jostling sprigs of willow lashed to the cabs.
They do not see, beneath them,
The peasants slanting back now toward their farms,
Wives twisting on their donkeys
To watch the city as it drops behind.

Barges begin now: the canal
Curves upward from the lower margin
Bearing a deckhand stretched in sleep
And a cook who fries fish.
The shops yawn open in air hazy with breakfast.
Four stevedores lug wheat from a barge—

The overseer disposes
His bulk already on the bags,
Waving his arm egregiously.

But soon the rainbow bridge, seething,
And one more span above a moat
To the great gate, while the canal
Loops outward to the upper margin.
The wines, cheeses, incense,
Rich fabrics, fortune tellers,
Medicines and samples of calligraphy
Decamp from the interiors,
From carts and quayside barges.
                                Always the barges,
Navigating with their spatula rudders
Or roped tightly to the bank each with its own winch,
Draw deeply, gravidly,
Bringing it in, all of it—
The ten thousand things
Arrange themselves upon
The hundred diagonals—
The brush strokes are strong, all of them,
Deep distance, penetrable space. . . .
Inside the vacant tower on the great gate
Hangs the alarm gong brilliant
From its leather braces.

Supply, provision, engorgement—
A triptych waxing on the sun's gradient,
Even as cart-wheel rims, foreshortened,
Stand wider at the tops than at the sides.
The eye that noticed this
Cannot be found in the ten
The twenty and the thirty versions
By all the bastard and the well-paid sons;
Chang dressed his customers and onlookers
In the rich sameness of prosperity

So as to drape their singleness of gesture.
Carts wallow multiple as noise
Passing the temple door
And cool stone feet of the Buddha
Lodged in the midmost of the shops and stalls.
In that finesse of the Constructive Art
He was not imitated.
His focus ends at a crossroads, at high noon;
He leaves one to imagine
The Imperial Palace
Farther on into late sun,
Canto on tiered canto
Bodiless, whole in splendor,
Picturable
But not pictured.

✑ IN FRONT OF A JAPANESE PHOTOGRAPH

A sentry and a ladder mark the wall,
But shadows only, on the open wood.
Its paint was burnt away, though not quite all:
It stands yet where the man and ladder stood.

Sun making second morning at ground zero
Had photographed them, silhouettes on white—
Matchstick rungs and the flat outline, no hero,
Of the single human shape, erect and slight.

He might have looked into the glare, or not.
We make out only, once again, the wood,
And shadows cast by nothing at that spot.
And looking, that we stand where he had stood.

4

✍ FOR THE ENGRAVER

Shall I say your thumb brushes my thumb,
That together we are thieves of time
And time's pieces, bending over them

With styluses, prying to possess
And reduce each of them to riches,
To make leafy the atomic rose?

The accomplishment of burglary
Lures us to the same scene unwary,
And we find, lifting the sash freely,

That the darkened house we penetrate
Is our own, and we our own secret,
And on the wall, dim, our own portrait

That hangs—we must take it with us now,
Our skill vague in our hands as shadow,
New stealth grainy as our lives, and go;

And, as the young Kathe Köllwitz did,
A harsh lamp near her head suspended,
Shadowing the tall jar of acid

And westering moon of her small face,
Turn a dark eye darkening toward us,
And then an eye blind with light as ice.

Her back humps into blackness, her hair
Draws back into the taut dark nowhere
That floats her table and composure

Around the focus of her calm hands
And the etched figure that burns there, tense,
Lifting up blackness in a black dance.

ᗭ POINTING

Old mortar powdering from older bricks:
I chiseled chunks out, heard the seated bone
Twisting on gristle after long disuse,
Consistency of stale bread, knife stuck deep.
Take out the old connective tissue, let
Air pack its ice around your buried gums,
Work till the evening like a soft eraser
Smudges the inessential: brick is rice paper,
Fishermen take the shore path into sky
Fogged limitless, T'ao-chi spread it like mortar—
Jade blades up to the midriff, over the path,
A gate half open; dusk dissolving creepers,
River village under the moon: dogs barking,
Fishermen file home, torches in their hands.

ℐ IN THE TWINKLING OF AN EYE

In Van Gogh's letters, one page is a match
Flaring to sulfur, ash, then back to paper:
It is the Belgian coalfields, midnight storm,
And in its flash he sees the huge Marcasse,
The mine, stranded in open fields, and sees
The ark, the perfect shipwreck. We see him,
His mind like film one passive moment, bright,
Containing all the landscape, all the sky,
The figures frozen to their shadows, glass
Lit in the windows though no lamps are lit,
Trees throwing spiders onto clapboard, then
All washed again in darkness, spiders left
To grope back toward their crevices and feed
Repetitively on the fire that fled.

✐ THE NAUTILUS

You look for some lost thing, then you forget,
Foraging brightness from the flow, the new.
And nautilus, chamber to chamber, builds
Around himself, sending back through the tubes
Into those rooms that curve to form his past
An acrid gas, that elevates his back
And bumps him on the filthy swirling floor
He feeds from. So his shell mouth blackens, ragged;
Room after room he chews the same discoveries,
Although his bobbing looks like graceful greed,
Mingled of indigestion and surprise.
Into the fireplace, absently, I poured
Old paper, then saw brilliant fingers hold
The thing I thought I'd lost, wilting from sight.

ℐ APPLE

Tithes, swags and filchings from the dark tree—
What have you thieved from your own body,
And by whose hand? Heartwood stiff already

In the stunning light, hardness is wise—
Slowly it trims distances with eyes
Rimming old prunings. They do not close,

They watch the boy's hand dart from below
For fruit, eyes to which his yet may grow;
Leaves fingering through his hands also,

Silk whispering shy of his ear's face;
The hand reaching would test nothing less
Than evil in its felt weightlessness,

Its perfect vacancy of motive—
So young Austin would have it, would have
The act itself smooth as an olive

Caught and stopped growing in his hand's heat:
Else he would have foreseen the panicked
Stirring of leaves he feels taking root

In his breathing, his eyes, his running
From himself or whatever new thing
He is: rings ripple, bark breaks, and hangs.

And the hand falls. Slowly, as you would
Shroud a child in sun-sleep unshielded,
Your body swims into wheat, toward shade

Of that tree forgotten, the theft so
Long forgotten; and whatever you
Have taken, it will precede you now,

Grass there will stoop in salutation,
Wind mantle you with it, worm glisten
With it; for only you have not known.

✍ DEVOTIONAL

My finger found the snug holes in your dial
And spun them idly—you were somewhere there—
Spun them again, dial purring all the while—

And let my hand ride backward on that purr,
Sleeping against the sprung return, slow arc
Over the ouija digits, luck's white blur,

Ticking its cricket language through the dark:
My finger nestled in each belly, mine
No longer, but some young boy's on a lark,

Riding the ferris wheel until my spine
Curled on its sickness in the windy glide,
The buzz of missed connections down the line.

I was him poking with my key inside
The same door pushing open every time—
Into this empty room, a keyhole wide

And spinning beneath me while the numbers roam
In order past the window, smooth and white—
Somewhere in here, you spin the tumblers home

With an old gesture, and turn on the light.

ℐ THE CHILDREN

I reached the town late that afternoon,
Walking. It was still: were they all in
The fields? But then I heard the children—

Over the rooftops came their light cries,
Leaves spiraling in wind, while houses
Slept on beneath them, masked certainties.

I followed through bent streets, but they fell
Quiet for a long while. Each new wall
And corner that I came to was full

Of the same shadow, the same light, points
Of each through each, as the raking glance
Over stucco withdrew brilliance.

Then I found them, kneeling close, intense,
Setting out their small braille of ear bones
On sweats of shadow, weaving a dance

With bird fingers that, from point to point,
Perfect in unspoken arrangement,
Kept their balance in the heavy slant

Of sun—their bodies small dark islands
In that uncut light. It cools their hands
Even as its radiance thickens.

✐ LEAVING THE COAL CELLAR

The wind lisps from its belly
Rehearsing the immunity of its names,
Slipping through nets of what is
Like shoals of small fish turning
With one intelligence,
Brightening one moment down
The million coins of their flanks,
Then darkening through weirs
Of the trees, leaving only
The tapering long wheeze of the recovering lung,
Cloud tumbling through it in a frieze of attitudes
Unfinished, hurrying toward completion—

I store another season's tools
Beneath the house and climb
Through sloping doors half-folded back like wings;
Emerge with cobweb face and hands
Into this wind laced suddenly
With the old hint that blood sacrifice
Of a young girl can raise wind again,
Out of death wrinkling the mirror
Silver to the sea's rim,
Lift canvas like these trees, humming again
With that swarm of bees death tunes and dances,
Oars leaping hammer-speed before the storm
Into their raid, then homeward with the wreck
Of pollen dangling in a favoring wind.

✐ SPRING JOURNEY

Whole from the mountain highway
As in sleep: trees gliding through themselves,
And then, where snow had sunk away,
Pool after pool in scattered shelves
Catching the image of the sun,
Rolling it deep inside the hill;
And flashes of this place again
Alive with hunters, and the kill,
And of Golaud, tracking fresh blood
Until he knew his way no more,
Coming on water in the wood,
And Melisande weeping there,
And far within that water, gold:
The crown that Bluebeard gave to her
Thrown to the bottom, blurred and cold.
And she refused to touch that crown,
Forbidding him to touch her flesh,
Urging that she must stay, alone;
Until Golaud, watching the mesh
Of gold weave deep within the pool,
Persuaded her that she must go
With him before the dark could fall,
With him, which way he did not know.

✒ THE TURN

Your neck, coiling to your bare shoulder,
Pulled itself tighter beneath warm hair—
And now that tension, like my future

Meeting me momently, advances
Its edge toward the still net of my gaze:
This is how recognition seizes,

How the patterns of obscure ruins
Reveal themselves to fliers, faint lines
Rising printlike through the grassy plains,

How war comes, blowing torn cloudshadows
Over the waking face of land, as
Suddenly the shapes of small countries

Shrivel like puddles under bald sun—
While, lost in time, slopes we might have known
Fold to wings of the rocked, sleeping tern,

Wedged at ease deep in the green day, where
Mushrooms drink the earth's secret color,
Steeping in the long noons toward summer.

✍ A QUARREL

It was no polished blade,
Nor the bright accidental blood,
   Nor even rock split clean
      By the green wedge
      Of saxifrage—

But more like March wind, heady
         And chill,
With sculls rehearsing for their race,
   Their crews hunched into place,
   One of them poised and still,
      Oars at the ready,
   Until another warily
Pulls even with it—
                  then together
They lunge out suddenly in step,
   Stroke and then feather,
   Accurate flash and dip
      Down their barked cadences.

𝒮 THE QUIET

Bent to your legs, undressing them,
Your back bends the light with it,
Warmly down and along
The spine's rivulet.

Then flexes it out to less than sheen
With your rising, gathering
All to contours, with the open
Secrets of odor.

Later, when the night rain has laced
Air with earth, grass, and the mixed
Pungencies of stone, there sounds
A patter, relaxed.

Warm void on waking, benevolent
Silence of this room becoming
Tiring-house to gestures,
The day's turnings

Idly wrought to the pitch of amendment.
You turn away in sleep, animal
Languor, a waterfall's smooth head,
Or hopes quieted—

It is hours until light arrives,
Lifts us out along some radius
From this hub, into the balanced
Exchange of lives.

Sleep, while off toward terminals a thrumming
Crosses gaps in the night wind—
The lean of whistles, not breaking,
And then, broken.

✒ VESTIBULE

All day our paths had crossed, I'd missed you twice
Or three times—then, had come home tired to find
Your sweater on the couch, your shoes kicked off,
The coffee still warm in your waiting cup—
And lightly called your name, only to hear it
Measure the silences; then felt my eyes
Stray back across the sweater's rich abandon,
The shoes more delicate for lying empty,
The porcelain zero of the cup—but then you called,
Upstairs and far away. Your voice brought back
Another room we entered once together,
Catching our breath—bare benches where the Shakers
Sat quiet after field work and prepared
To go together to the larger room.

✍ DARK ON DARK

Fireflies heavier after rain, gold
Flaring green, god and mortal mingled—
Come, look with me over the whole field,

They surround us, swinging and lifting
Apostrophes on dusk, while words hang
Shy of speech: *those you love will live long*—

Presences through haze, needing no voice,
They widen through our wake in wet grass,
With hid roots tug vanishing at us—

Leaving touch as our child leaves us—as
Even now strength sieves and the light goes
As to a strange place. Yet it shadows

Some familiar experience,
The way pages half possess our hands,
Filtering through fingers till sense thins

Into that large hand round us, dusk full
Upon the whole unremarkable
Mask of memory, air threading cool.

Where odor interleaves with odor,
Dark on dark, there you wait, your finger
Marking place while the head lifts once more,

Soft cone rinsing inward, and inward,
Light spiraling in dregs round the slurred
Center—the recognized, retreating word.